FUNdamental
Science

Key Stage 1

Everyday Materials

by Ruth Owen

Published in 2016 by Ruby Tuesday Books Ltd.

Editor: Mark J. Sachner
Designer: Emma Randall
Consultant: Judy Wearing, PhD, BEd
Production: John Lingham

Photo credits:
Alamy: 11, 17 (top), 17 (bottom), 20 (centre), 20 (bottom), 21 (top), 25 (bottom), 27 (top); Getty Images: 10 (top), 10 (bottom), 16 (bottom); Shutterstock: Cover, 1, 2–3, 4–5, 6–7, 8–9, 10 (centre), 12–13, 14–15, 16 (top), 17 (centre), 18–19, 20 (top), 21 (bottom), 22–23, 24, 25 (top), 26, 27 (centre), 27 (bottom), 28–29, 30–31.

British Library Cataloguing in Publication Data (CIP)
is available for this title.

ISBN 978-1-910549-85-8

Printed in China by Toppan Leefung

www.rubytuesdaybooks.com

Contents

Words shown in **bold** in the text are explained in the glossary.

The download button shows there are free worksheets or other resources available. Go to:

www.rubytuesdaybooks.com/scienceKS1

What Are Materials?

All around us there are lots of objects and they are all made from materials.

The pictures on this page show different materials.

Wool

Wood

Glass

Plastic

Metal

Rock

A material is something that can be made into something else.

What materials are the objects on this page made from?

Marbles

Spoon

Glove

Can you match each object to one of the materials on page 4?

(The answers are at the bottom of the page.)

Playing cards

Toy bricks

Bowl

Statue

Answers: The toy bricks are plastic; the statue is made of rock; the glove is made of wool; the dog bowl is metal; the marbles are glass; the spoon and playing cards are made from wood.

Let's Investigate Properties

Materials have properties that we use to describe them such as rough or smooth, dull or shiny.

See-through plastic bottle

plastic cups not see-through

Smooth, shiny metal spoon

Rough, dull rock

The objects made from a material can have these properties, too.

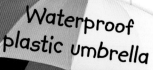

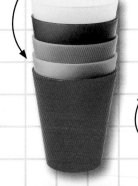

Waterproof plastic umbrella

Cardboard box not waterproof

Stretchy rubber balloon

Stiff wooden pencil

Bendy rubber hose

Tools not bendy

Wood

Metal

Let's Investigate!

When scientists describe a material as "hard", it means it is difficult to scratch. A material that's described as "soft" is easy to scratch. Let's investigate!

What happens if you scratch the glass in a window with your fingernail?

What happens if you scratch a piece of chalk?

Which material is hard and which is soft?

(The answers are at the bottom of the page.)

A waterproof material does not let water soak into it. A material that's **absorbent** soaks up water.

Absorbent fabric towel

Rubber tyre not absorbent

Answer: You probably left no mark on the glass when you scratched it. That's because glass is a hard material. Chalk is a soft material so you were able to scratch it and leave a mark.

7

Wood from Nature

Some materials come from nature. Wood is a natural material that comes from trees.

A tree is cut down

Wooden logs

Trees for wood are grown in huge forests.

Wood is delivered to factories or workshops to be made into wooden objects.

Wood can be cut or **carved** into different shapes.

Lolly stick

Furniture

Carved wooden owl

Let's Talk

Can you find five things made from wood in your home or classroom?

One of the properties of wood is that it is strong. A strong material is difficult to break.

Wooden building

Making Paper

Paper is also a natural material that is made from trees.

Logs at a paper mill

Fibres

At a paper mill logs are crushed into tiny pieces called fibres.

The fibres are mixed with water to make a porridge-like mixture called pulp.

Pulp

Newly made wet paper

On a giant paper-making machine the pulp is rolled and squeezed.

The water is removed and it becomes flat paper.

Let's Talk

How many different ways do you use paper?

Roll of paper

After the paper is dried and rolled up, it is ready to leave the factory.

Let's Investigate Paper

We use paper every day in lots of different ways.

Books

Toilet roll

Crafts

Notebooks

Wrapping paper

Newspapers and magazines

Cardboard is a type of thick paper that's also made from trees.

Sometimes very thick cardboard is made by glueing together layers of paper.

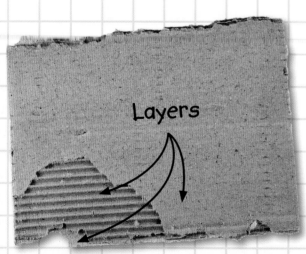
Layers

Try looking at some cardboard and paper through a magnifying glass. Can you see the tiny wood fibres?

Be a Scientist!

Let's investigate some of the properties and uses of paper.
Draw a chart to record your results.

Gather your equipment:
- Six samples of paper
- A small square object with hard corners
- Sticky tape
- Scissors
- A saucer
- Some water
- A ruler
- A notebook and pen

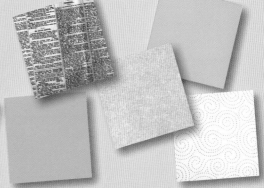

Is all paper suitable for wrapping gifts?

Try wrapping your square object in each paper sample.

How suitable is each type of paper for this job? Record your results.

Not suitable Suitable Very suitable

How are the suitable paper samples different from the others?

	Wrapping Gifts Results	Absorbent or Not Absorbent
Toilet paper		
Kitchen roll		
Wrapping paper		
Printer paper		
Greaseproof paper		
Newspaper		

Is paper absorbent or not absorbent?

1. Cut a strip of each paper that's 15 cm long and 3 cm wide. Lay one end of each strip in the saucer.

2. Carefully pour some water into the saucer so it touches each strip. Observe what happens.

How far up the strip does the water soak? Record your results in centimetres.

Which paper is most absorbent? Which is least absorbent?

How is the most absorbent paper different to the others?

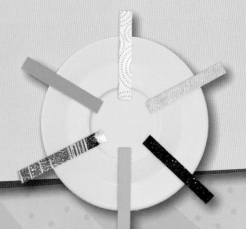

Rock in Our World

Rock from mountains, cliffs and under the ground is used by people in many ways.

Rock for building is dug from a huge hole in the ground called a quarry.

Quarry

Rock

At a quarry, workers set off explosions to break the rock into giant pieces. Then machines cut it into smaller blocks for building.

People use rock to build houses, schools and other buildings.

Rock

Rock is crushed and mixed with water and other materials to make concrete.

Concrete is used to build apartment blocks, bridges, roads and pavements.

Where Does Metal Come From?

Some metals, such as iron and aluminium, are natural materials found in rock.

Steel is a metal that people make out of iron.

At a huge factory called a steel plant, iron is mixed with coal and a rock called limestone.

This rock contains iron.

Furnace

The mixture goes into a scorching-hot oven called a **furnace**.

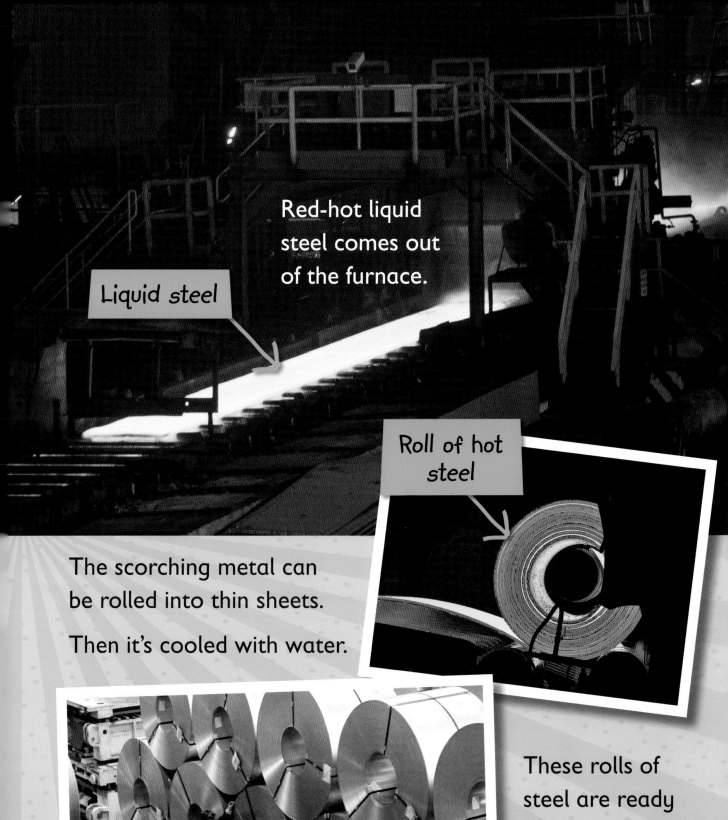

Red-hot liquid steel comes out of the furnace.

Liquid *steel*

Roll of hot steel

The scorching metal can be rolled into thin sheets.

Then it's cooled with water.

These rolls of steel are ready to be made into metal objects.

A roll of steel may be up to a kilometre long.

How We Use Metals

Metal can be hard, shiny or strong. These properties make it a suitable material to make many objects.

Steel is used to make the frameworks of tall buildings, such as The Shard in London.

It is also used to make cars and lorries.

The Shard

Keys

Aluminium is a metal that is found in rock.

It is used for making planes, drinks cans, keys and aluminium foil.

Plane

Cans

Foil

Coins are made from mixtures of different metals including copper and nickel.

Let's Talk

Glass is a material that is made by people. What do you think it's made of?

Making Glass

Glass is made from a mixture of sand and special **chemicals**.

At a glass factory the mixture is melted in a furnace.

Scorching-hot melted glass

Glass horse

The melted glass can be shaped to make bowls, glasses, animals and other objects.

When the glass cools down, it is hard and **transparent**, or see-through.

In glass factories, melted glass is made into bottles and jars.

These glass bottles are still scorching hot.

It's also made into thin, flat sheets for making windows and doors.

Let's Talk

Why is glass a good material to make windows from?

(The answer is at the bottom of the page.)

Answer: Glass lets light into buildings and allows people inside to see out. It is also waterproof so it keeps out rain.

Plastic in Our World

Plastic is produced by people in factories. It is made from oil, coal, chemicals and other materials.

Plastic can be thick, thin, bendy or stiff.

Plastic objects can be made in any shape or colour.

Plastic can be transparent or **opaque**.

Transparent goggles

Opaque suitcase

22

Plastic can even be used to make fabrics for clothes.

Stretchy lycra leotard

Waterproof raincoat

 Let's Explore!

Go on a plastic treasure hunt in your home or school.

Can you find the following objects?

- A plastic object that's bendy.

- A plastic object that's opaque.

- A plastic object that's transparent.

- An object that's part plastic and part wood.

- An object that's part plastic and part metal.

These tiny beads are pellets of plastic. In factories the pellets are heated and melted. Then the melted plastic can be shaped into different objects.

Bouncy, Bendy Rubber

Rubber is a stretchy, bendy material that comes from rubber trees.

Rubber bands

Rubber gloves

Rubber tree

Sap

Cup

On a rubber tree farm, a worker makes a cut in a rubber tree's bark.

A sticky, white liquid called **sap** flows from the cut into a cup.

Rubber sheets

A chemical is added to the sap to make it thicken.

Then the thickened sap is rolled into sheets – like rubbery dough.

Rubber that comes from trees is a natural material. People can also make rubber from oil and chemicals.

The rubber sheets are sent to factories to make objects such as tyres, balloons, gloves and rubber bands.

Tyre

Materials for Clothes

The clothes we wear are made of fabrics. To make fabric, thin threads are woven or knitted together.

Some fabrics, such as polyester, are made from plastics.

Others, such as cotton, are made from natural materials.

Polyester football shirt

Cotton

Cotton plants

Fluffy, white cotton grows on plants. Cotton is used to make fabric for jeans, T-shirts and other clothes.

Wool is a natural material that comes from animals such as sheep and alpacas.

Fleece

Fleece

Alpaca

This alpaca is having its woolly fleece sheared off. It doesn't hurt the animal.

Ball of wool

Knitted scarf

The fleece is **dyed** different colours and spun into thread called wool, or yarn.

Then it can be knitted into jumpers, hats and scarves.

Let's Test It!

Now it's time to try out everything you've discovered.

Garden path

Pencil sharpener

Envelope

Magnifying glass

Kitchen sponge

Boots

Spectacles

Tights

Let's Talk

What materials do you think the objects on these pages are made of?

(The answers are at the bottom of the page.)

Box

Matches

Answers: Matches are wood; pencil sharpener is metal and plastic; garden path is rock; boots are rubber; tights are nylon, which is a type of plastic; spectacles, or glasses, are glass with metal frames; sponge is plastic; box is cardboard; envelope is paper; magnifying glass is plastic, metal and glass.

29

Recycling Materials

Objects made from paper, plastic and glass can often be recycled.

Recycled objects can become materials for making new objects.

Instead of using paint, this picture was created using plastic bottle tops.

Instead of using rock, this statue was made
from old plastic bottles.

Let's **Explore!**

We choose materials carefully to do different jobs.
Look at these three objects.

Chocolate
teapot

Cardboard
truck

Hammer
made of jelly

Why are the materials unsuitable to make these objects?

What problems would there be if these objects were used?

What materials are a better choice?

Glossary

absorbent
Able to soak up liquid.

carve
To cut and shape a material, such as wood or rock to make statues or ornaments.

chemical
A substance that comes from nature or is made by people. Chemicals can be used to produce materials such as plastic.

dye
To change the colour of a material using chemicals called dyes. Materials such as wool and plastic can be dyed.

furnace
An extremely hot oven in a factory, used for melting metals or other materials. The temperature in a furnace may be higher than 1000°C.

opaque
Not able to be seen through.

sap
The liquid inside a plant that carries nutrients and water throughout the plant.

transparent
Allowing light to pass through.

Index